The Singing Giant

A Play

Margaret Ryan
Illustrated by Jonathan Langley

The Characters

Narrator

George the Giant

Mum

Grandpa

Baby

Sister

Scene One

Narrator: We are in George the Giant's house.

George: I love to sing. I love to sing.
I sing in the morning,
I sing in the evening,
I sing in the bath.
Tra, la, la.

Scene Two

Narrator: We are now in the house next door.

George: *I LOVE TO SING. I LOVE TO SING.*

Mum: Stop that singing.
I can't sleep at night.

Grandpa: Stop that singing.
I can't sleep in the morning.

Sister: Stop that singing.
I can't hear the television.

George: *I LOVE TO SING.*
HOW I LOVE TO SING.
TRA LA LA LA LA.

Mum: George must stop singing.

Sister: Yes, we have to stop him making so much noise.

Grandpa: Let's go and see him.

Scene Three

Narrator: We are now at George's house again.

George: Hello, everyone. Nice to see you. Have you come to hear me sing?

Everyone: No, we have not!

Mum: We have come to tell you to stop singing.

Grandpa: Yes, I can't sleep because of all the noise.

Sister: And I can't hear the television because of all the noise.

Everyone: You must stop singing, George.

George: But I love to sing. Ohhhh. Sniffle, sniffle.

Scene Four

Narrator: We are now next door again.

Mum: Listen, it's very quiet.

Grandpa: Now I can sleep.

Sister: Now I can hear the television.

Everyone: Peace and quiet at last. *Sigh.*

Baby: *WAAAAA!*
WAAAAAA!
WAAAAAA!

Scene Five

Narrator: It is now the next morning.

Baby: *WAAA! WAAA! WAAA!*

Mum: I didn't sleep a wink all night. Yawn.

Grandpa: I didn't sleep at all. Yawn.

Sister: I couldn't hear the television and I couldn't sleep! Yawn.

Baby: *WAAA! WAAA! WAAA!*

Mum: Maybe if we rock the baby, the baby will stop crying.

Grandpa: Maybe if we take the baby for a walk, the baby will stop crying.

Sister: Maybe if we play with the baby, the baby will stop crying.

Baby: *WAAAAAAAAAAAAAAAAAAAA!*

Everyone: PLEASE STOP CRYING!

Sister: The baby didn't cry when George was singing.

Mum: Oh! You're right! When George sang, the baby slept.

Grandpa: We must go to see George again.

Scene Six

Narrator: We are at George's house again.

George: Hello, I'm not singing now.

Everyone: Please start singing again, George.
The baby loves your singing.
We're sorry we asked you to stop.

Baby: Gurgle, gurgle. Sing song.

George: You really mean it? You want me to sing again? FANTASTIC!
I'll sing my favourite song.

George: SLEEP LITTLE BABY, DON'T YOU CRY . . .

Baby: Zzzz Zzzz Zzzz . . .

Everyone: Bravo, George! Bravo!